Sermon Outlines
on
Lessons
from the
Early Church

GENE WILLIAMS

Beacon Hill Press of Kansas City
Kansas City, Missouri

Copyright 2002
By Beacon Hill Press of Kansas City

ISBN 083-411-9919

Printed in the
United States of America

Cover Design: Paul Franitza

Unless otherwise indicated, all Scripture quotations are taken from the *Holy Bible, New International Version*® (NIV®). Copyright © 1973, 1978, 1984 by International Bible Society. Used by permission of Zondervan Publishing House. All rights reserved.

Permission to quote from the following additional copyrighted versions is acknowledged with appreciation:

The Bible: A New Translation (MOFFATT). Copyright 1922, 1924, 1925, 1935 by Harper and Row, Publishers, Incorporated. Copyright 1950, 1952, 1953, 1954 by James A. R. Moffatt.

New American Standard Bible® (NASB®), © copyright The Lockman Foundation 1960, 1962, 1963, 1968, 1971, 1972, 1973, 1975, 1977, 1995.

The Living Bible (TLB), © 1971. Used by permission of Tyndale House Publishers, Inc., Wheaton, IL 60189. All rights reserved.

Scripture quotations marked KJV are from the King James Version.

Library of Congress Cataloging-in-Publication-Data

Williams, Gene, 1932-
  Sermon outlines on lessons from the early church / Gene Williams.
    p. cm. — (Beacon sermon outline series)
  ISBN 0-8341-1991-9 (pbk.)
  1. Bible. N.T. Acts—Sermons—Outlines, syllabi, etc. 2. Bible. N.T. Epistles—Sermons—Outlines, syllabi, etc. I. Title. II. Series.
  BS2617.5 .W55 2002
  251'.02—dc21
                                                          2002009483

10 9 8 7 6 5 4 3 2 1

Sermon Outlines on Lessons from the Early Church

Contents

Introduction: Messages from the Early Church   7
1. The Lord's Provision (Acts 1:1-11)   9
2. Obedient People Have Special Experiences (Acts 1:4; 2:1-8)   11
3. Helping a Needy World (Acts 3:1-10)   13
4. No Reason to Run Out (Acts 4:23-31)   15
5. The Game Is Over (Acts 5:1-11)   17
6. A Lesson in Divine Providence (Acts 5:12-42)   19
7. Two Lessons We Must Learn (Acts 6:1-15; 7:54-60)   21
8. Lifting Up Jesus (Acts 8:1-13)   23
9. No Impossible Cases (Acts 9:1-19)   25
10. The Anatomy of a Happy Home (Acts 10:1-8, 19-25)   27
11. The People Called Christians (Acts 11:19-26)   29
12. Celebration of Freedom (Acts 12:1-16)   31
13. The Key to Great Joy (Acts 13:1-12, 44-52)   33
14. The Good News Passed On (Acts 13:32-48)   35
15. The Place of the Church in Today's World (Acts 15:1-21)   37
16. Lessons from Philippi (Acts 16:16-40)   39
17. Christianity Simplified (Acts 16:25-34)   41
18. A Second Work of Grace (Acts 19:1-7)   43
19. The Great Change That Jesus Brings (Acts 26:1-19)   45
20. Lessons from Paul (Acts 26:1-19)   47
21. Four Anchors (Acts 27:13-36)   49
22. Finding a Place of Safety (Acts 27:33-44)   51
23. The Life That Really Matters (Galatians 2:11-20)   53
24. A Choice to Make (Galatians 5:16-26)   55
25. A Magnificent Obsession (Philippians 1:21; 3:7-11)   57
26. Press On (Philippians 3:7-21)   59
27. Faith in Daily Living (James 2:14-26)   61
28. Sinners, Servants, or Sons? (Romans 8:12-17)   63

Introduction

Messages from the Early Church

The Early Church turned its world upside down. It spread the good news of Jesus in the face of extremely hostile conditions. And the Church made an impression on its world. Some of these messages will come from individuals such as Paul. Others will come from the Church body. Taking a close look at the Church as recorded in the Book of Acts can teach us much about how to spread the Good News in our world. We will also learn from some of the Epistles.

A person may use these messages in series or lift one or more of them out of the set for emphasis on a special truth. They are simple truths from ordinary but committed people who determined that they would not allow anything to turn them aside.

Some of the messages will present a challenge to the modern Church. Others will encourage and inspire as we see how God helped those early believers through some very trying circumstances.

Take these simple seeds of truth, plant them in your fertile mind, water them with prayer, add some personal touches, and see what God brings forth.

The Lord's Provision

Acts 1:1-11

Introduction
- A. Jesus understood the needs of His disciples before they knew they had a problem.
  1. He was preparing them for the trying days He knew were ahead.
  2. He was making provision for them so that they could continue to live victorious lives.
- B. The nature of people has not changed.
  1. We may not experience that which precipitated the disciples' crisis. We experience the same needs.
  2. It is important to understand that He who provided for them will also provide for us.
- C. Our scripture illuminates three areas of life in which believers would be inadequate if it were not for Jesus' provision.
- D. Read the scripture, Acts 1:1-11.

I. He Provided Them Proof of the Resurrection (v. 3)
- A. It would be important that they had no doubts about the Resurrection. Everything Christianity teaches depends on its validity.
  1. Paul declared, "If Christ has not been raised, then our preaching is vain" (1 Cor. 15:14, NASB).
  2. Jesus knew how vital it would be that all questions were removed.
- B. The proof is infallible (Acts 1:3).
  1. There are 6 documented appearances.
  2. Paul lists them in 1 Cor. 15.
  3. The enemies of Jesus only needed to produce His body.
- C. The followers were so convinced that they became an irresistible force.
  1. They practiced all He had taught them.

2. Unqualified belief in the Resurrection enables us to live up to our potential as Christians.

II. He Provided Them Power to Carry Out Their Assignment (Acts 1:8)
   A. Jesus assigned believers to live in such a way that the rest of the world would have a reason to believe in Him.
      1. This meant they would live in peace, purity, and pleasure.
      2. This meant the world could see Jesus living through the lives of those who believed in Him.
      3. In order to do this they would need the power that would be given in Acts 2.
   B. Our assignment is the same today.
      1. We are the only "Jesus" many people will ever see.
      2. The presence of the Holy Spirit manifested in the lives of believers means that the struggling world is exposed to the truth about Jesus.

III. He Provided the Confidence to Believe in a Beautiful Future (Acts 1:11)
   A. This confidence in heaven would stimulate the disciples to live fearlessly.
      1. Jesus describes heaven in John 14 and Rev. 20—21.
      2. Knowing that there is another life enabled them to keep the faith.
   B. The assurance of heaven should enable us to live confident lives today.
      1. No one who is thinking clearly would choose to miss heaven.
      2. Remember that the provisions are offered to all believers.

Conclusion
   A. Jesus' proof of the Resurrection, power for daily living, and promise of a future with Him continue to enable today's Church to live victoriously in a fallen world.
   B. That provision gave Paul the confidence that he expresses in 2 Tim. 4:7-8.

Obedient People Have Special Experiences

Acts 1:4; 2:1-8

Introduction
- A. God has wonderful plans for people who are obedient to Him.
  1. Look at Isa. 1:19, Hab. 1:5, and Jer. 29:11-13.
  2. To enjoy His plans, we must be obedient to His will.
- B. The scripture for today focuses on the people of the Early Church.
  1. Read Acts 1:2-4; 2:1-8.
  2. Their option was to obey and wait or to get busy on their own.
  3. 120 believers obeyed and waited.
  4. We wonder what happened to those who left rather than obey the Lord's command to wait.
- C. We are going to look at the special experience that came to those who waited as Jesus had instructed.

I. It Was an Emotional Time Unlike Any Anyone Had Ever Experienced
- A. The Holy Spirit swept over them in an overwhelming manifestation.
  1. Note verses 2:2-4, 12, 15-21.
  2. Is it good to experience such emotion?
  3. We accept emotional experiences in every other area of our lives.
- B. Obedient Christians have a warm feeling toward God.
  1. They are open and responsive to His movement.
  2. Disobedient people are afraid that they give away their true selves.
  3. Could our world be waiting for people who are willing to turn God loose in their lives?

II. It Was a Mystical Experience (vv. 5-8)
- A. Some things cannot be explained or understood. They can only be experienced.

     1. In verse 6 we read how those present understood in their own languages the words of the disciples.
     2. Obedient people enjoy the workings of God.
  B. Wherever God moves, some mystery is involved.
     1. In Job 5:9 we read, "He performs wonders that cannot be fathomed."
     2. The Israelites did not understand the destruction of Jericho.
  C. Obedient people have unforgettable experiences.

III. It Was a Melting Moment (Acts 2:1-11)
  A. These obedient people were blended together in a very special way.
  B. Obedient people are so focused on their relationship with God that they easily relate to others.
     1. They experienced wonderful fellowship (vv. 42-47).
     2. Obedient people love one another.

IV. A Movement Was Born
  A. These obedient people started a movement that has affected the entire world.
     1. It was the birthday of the Church.
     2. They grew dramatically.
  B. The movement was powerful.
     1. In verse 43, 46-47 we read that the world took notice of them.
     2. God's blessings are in proportion to our obedience.
     3. As modern-day believers become obedient, we, too, will experience special times with God.

Conclusion
  A. Obedience does not always lead us down a comfortable path.
  B. Obedient people have special experiences about which others only dream.
  C. God is looking for some people who will allow Him to have His way in their lives.

Helping a Needy World

Acts 3:1-10

Introduction
- A. The Book of Acts tells us in simple terms how the Early Church functioned and affected its world.
- B. We are going to look at an interesting experience in the life of the young Church.

I. It Will Help Us Understand What Has Brought the Church to This Point
- A. The believers had been given a command and two promises (see chap. 1).
  1. The command was to tarry in Jerusalem (see v. 4).
  2. Promise No. 1 was that they would receive the Holy Spirit (see v. 5).
  3. Promise No. 2 was, "This same Jesus . . . will come back" (v. 11).
- B. While they waited for the Second Coming, they were to live lives full of victory and joy.
  1. To do this they would have to be obedient to God's guidance.
  2. In chapter 2, the believers were obedient and God flooded over them through His wonderful Spirit.
  3. Please note: The Holy Spirit is not an "it." The Holy Spirit is *Him*—God's special way of being with His people.
- C. When we surrender our wills totally to Him, we enter into the life promised in Isa. 1:19.
- D. Many Christians struggle in an attempt to be good and are even exhausted by their efforts because they have never truly surrendered their wills to His way. In too many lives the clay is trying to dictate to the Potter what it wants to be (see Jer. 18).
- E. Read the Scripture, Acts 3:1-10.

II. The Obedient Believers Are Praying
   A. Twice we see the importance of prayer in the Early Church.
      1. In chapter 1 they were praying.
      2. Here, in chapter 3, they are on their way to a prayer meeting.
   B. The encounter mentioned in verses 2 and 3 would have been very normal.
      1. Before his encounter with the people of God the beggar was totally helpless.
      2. What happened after that encounter made him a completely different person.
      3. In verse 4 Peter and John are not timid survivors.
      4. They have absolute confidence according to verse 6.
   C. Peter did not give the man what he requested. He gave him what he needed.
      1. We live in a crippled world that needs help.
      2. Jesus can and will change the world if we will present Him.
   D. It is not silver and gold that the world needs. The world needs Jesus.

III. The World Needs Someone to Reach Out a Hand of Faith to the People
   A. It took faith to do what they did in verse 7.
   B. When believers reach out in faith, great things happen (see v. 8).
   C. When believers start living in a way that demonstrates what they say is true, a struggling world will find the help needed.
   D. The need today is for Christians to live the Spirit-filled life and reach out to a needy world.

Conclusion
   A. God will do mighty things to change crippled lives in our world when we fully trust Him.
   B. The miracles that are recorded in the Book of Acts can be repeated today if we become an obedient people.

No Reason to Run Out

Acts 4:23-31

Introduction
- A. Have you ever run out of gas?
  1. It can be embarrassing.
  2. It can be inconvenient.
- B. Nothing is more embarrassing or dangerous than believers running out of the fuel of the Holy Spirit.
- C. The believers in the Book of Acts learned quickly the lesson of needing a refilling.
  1. Time had passed since Pentecost and that great initial experience.
  2. As they have gone about the business of living Christian lives, much spiritual fuel has been expended.
  3. They recognized their need and came to the right place for help.
  4. Read the scripture, Acts 4:23-31.

I. They were pulling a heavy load.
- A. They did not take the blessings of God and hold on to them selfishly (see chap. 3).
  1. Note the healing of the crippled beggar in verse 6.
  2. They were passing on to others what God had given to them.
  3. They shared the Good News (see Peter's message in vv. 11-26).
- B. They were standing firm in the face of stiff opposition.
  1. Look at 4:1-10.
  2. Illustration: When we are pulling a heavy load, it takes a lot of fuel.
- C. It takes a lot of spiritual fuel to keep going in our world.
  1. The more danger we are to Satan, the more opposition we will receive from him.
  2. Take courage when he opposes you. He is afraid of your influence.

II. They Realized Their Need for God's Strength
    A. These believers were aware of their need for God's help.
        1. Note verse 29. They did not ask Him to remove the problem but to enable them to face it.
        2. If God removed their pressure, they would have no need of His presence within.
    B. These believers had proper priorities (v. 30).
        1. They could have accomplished something on their own but needed Him to make an impact.
        2. They became His channels of blessing to a struggling world (v. 33).

III. God Responded to Their Request (vv. 31-33)
    A. It was just like Pentecost again.
        1. God is not limited to a particular time or place.
        2. God is deeply committed to those who want Him (Isa. 65:24).
        3. No one ever has to beg to be filled.
    B. We endanger our effectiveness when we fail to seek Him.
        1. Sometimes we forget that after our crisis experience we still need fuel to keep going.
        2. We cannot store up enough fuel ahead of time to get us through life.

Conclusion
    A. There is no reason for anyone to run out of spiritual fuel.
        1. If you use up what you have, He will give you more.
        2. If you recognize your need for God's help, He will give it to you.
        3. God will respond just as He did for the believers in Acts 4:31.
    B. The station is open. This could be your day for a fresh filling.

The Game Is Over

Acts 5:1-11

Introduction
A. As children many of us played a game called let's pretend.
B. Unfortunately, many continue to play let's pretend spiritually long after the time for games is over.
C. In Acts 5 we are given the account of two people who played the game of pretending to be Christians.
   1. It is one of the most dramatic stories in the New Testament.
   2. The story vividly demonstrates the high price of hypocrisy.
   3. Read the scripture, Acts 5:1-11.

I. The Act of Deception
A. Why was the land sold in the first place?
   1. Barnabas had sold a piece of land and had brought the money to the apostles (4:36-37).
   2. This act of commitment and dedication had, no doubt, been exciting to the young Church.
   3. Ananias and Sapphira had witnessed the excitement that this gift had brought to the Church.
   4. Their problem began with their envying of the response to Barnabas's generous offering.
B. God had been good to Ananias and Sapphira.
   1. They were significant people in their community.
   2. Ananias literally meant "one to whom Jehovah has been gracious."
   3. Obviously, God had blessed them, and he was a man who had done good things.
C. The lesson is clear. God is not impressed with what we have or how good we are.
   1. He is not impressed with what others think of us but what is happening inside us.
   2. The more respect we receive from others, the more God expects of us.

D. They deceived themselves.
      1. They sold the property on their own initiative (5:1).
      2. They conspired together to deceive the Church (v. 2).
      3. Their gift to the Church was made as if it were complete.
      4. They may have given more than Barnabas, but that was not the point.
   E. If God struck down all of those who pretended to be totally committed to the Kingdom, we would see many empty places.
      1. People can be easily fooled.
      2. God is never fooled.

II. The Discovery of the Deception (vv. 3-4)
   A. Peter was prompted to make the examination. The Holy Spirit most likely gave him a special discernment.
      1. There are similar stories in the Old Testament.
      2. The story of Achan (Josh. 7—confronted by Joshua).
      3. David and Bathsheba (2 Sam. 11—confronted by Nathan).
   B. The lesson is crystal clear—God knows everything that is going on in our lives.
      1. Gal. 6:7
      2. Eccles. 12:14
      3. Matt. 12:14-16
      4. Rom. 2:16
   C. We do not deceive God. We can only deceive ourselves.

III. The Price of Deception Is High
   A. Look at what happened to Ananias (Acts 5:5).
   B. Look at what happened to Sapphira (v. 10).
   C. The Bible gives the clear picture that we cannot deceive God.

Conclusion
   A. This is no time for pretending or playing games.
   B. God did not let the Early Church members play games. Neither will He allow us to do so.

A Lesson in Divine Providence

Acts 5:12-42

Introduction
  A. There was never a dull moment around old Jerusalem First Church!
     1. Pentecost came in a blaze of glory (chap. 2).
     2. Healings occurred (the man at Temple gate, chapter 3).
     3. There were lessons on hypocrisy (5:1-11).
     4. The wave of power was building within the Church to a great climax.
  B. The Church today must learn to live like the Early Church in Jerusalem.
     1. We will have times when we almost seem to be invincible.
     2. We will have times when nothing seems to go right.
     3. The key to being what we need to be is to remember who we are.
  C. This is the overwhelming lesson of Acts 5:12-42. Read the scripture.

I. The Church Soaring (vv. 12-16)
  A. The Church was respected throughout the city (v. 13).
     1. Something in the Church members' lives made them believable.
     2. The reputation of individual members contributes to or detracts from the message of the Church.
  B. The Church was growing daily (v. 14).
     1. Whether the Church kept records or not, the Holy Spirit kept up with what was happening.
     2. When the Church soars, it is attractive to the people who are watching.
  C. The Church was a blessing to the community (vv. 15-16).
     1. People find a way to get where something good is happening.

2. Where the Spirit of the Lord is, there is something so attractive that distance is not a problem.

II. The Church Suffering (vv. 17-26)
   A. When we move into enemy territory, we can expect opposition.
   B. The Early Church faced opposition.
      1. Look at verses 18, 33, 40.
      2. Stephen paid with his life (Acts 7).
      3. The apostle Paul paid dearly.

III. The Church Surviving (5:19-20, 34)
   A. God will protect His property. Sometimes He does this in ways beyond our imagination (v. 19).
   B. Several lessons are worth learning.
      1. The Lord will not totally crush our opposition.
      2. God's people will not be immune to trials and setbacks.
      3. While there is opposition, nothing can stop the gospel's progress.
      4. The message of Jesus is more important than our comfort.

IV. The Church Singing (vv. 41-42)
   A. How did they maintain their joy?
      1. They were uncompromisingly obedient to God's will (v. 29).
      2. They had no questions about their message (vv. 30-32).
      3. They had the internal testimony of the Holy Spirit.
   B. So, they kept singing.

Conclusion
   A. The rough experience had induced no traces of doubt or indecision in the hearts of the apostles. They wore their wounds as badges of honor.
   B. God gave the song, and nothing could take that song away from those who kept the faith.
   C. Divine providence is the exciting reality for those who make a total commitment of their lives to Jesus Christ.

Two Lessons We Must Learn

Acts 6:1-15; 7:54-60

Introduction
- A. The Church has displayed its ability to handle the opposition of a hostile world.
  1. Remember 5:40-42.
  2. Spirit-filled people have an internal disposition that enables them not only to survive the opposition from the world but also to find a real sense of satisfaction about who they are in Christ (v. 41).
- B. That's why the membership growth in 6:1 happened then and will happen today. When we live lives that are filled with joy, the world will be attracted to Jesus.
  1. Sometimes the Church is its own worst enemy. Internal problems can come as a result of the growth and influx of new people.
  2. Read the scripture, Acts 6:1-15; 7:54-60.

I. Lesson No. 1: Even Spirit-Filled Churches Can Have Problems
- A. The word translated "complained" in the NIV and "murmuring" in the KJV comes from the Greek word that suggests the "buzzing of bees."
  1. There was a buzzing of complaints because some were not getting the attention they felt they deserved.
  2. In that day the only help widows received was from the Church.
- B. The Church faced its problem in a sanctified manner.
  1. The people were willing to make adjustments in their lives.
  2. Their compliance resolved the problem.
- C. The alternative to having this type of problem is to not grow.
  1. Most Christians would rather grow and deal with the resulting problems.

2. When the Church responded in a way that demonstrated that Jesus had made a difference in their lives, "the word of God spread" (v. 7).

II. Lesson No. 2: God Gives His People Special Strength to Face Difficult Situations
   A. The political powers of that period became unhappy with what was happening.
      1. Any time we invade the enemy's territory, he strikes back.
      2. Note verses 8-15.
   B. Stephen's simple message of Jesus and demonstration of God's presence upset the religious powers of that day.
      1. The synagogue had a very structured role in the community.
      2. When Stephen poured new wine into old wineskins, the synagogue members could not handle that.
      3. Religion can be a comforting experience, and the synagogue offered that comfort.
      4. Christianity makes us uncomfortable with what sin has done to our world.
   C. Stephen dared to upset the religious world of his day.
      1. According to verse 11, they had no scruples.
      2. Stephen's inner being shone through (v. 15).
      3. He dared to make them feel guilty (7:51).
   D. The straight truth as worded in 7:51 will almost always bring violent results.
      1. The result was that they killed Stephen (v. 54-60).
      2. People who die in the Spirit die well.
      3. John Wesley is quoted to have said, "Our people die well."

Conclusion
   A. One observer's life was changed forever (7:58).
      1. Saul (Paul) saw something in Stephen that he could never forget.
      2. Note verses 59-60.
   B. Two questions are appropriate.
      1. Does anyone see Jesus in you?
      2. Are you living a Christian life or a religious life?

Lifting Up Jesus

Acts 8:1-13

Introduction
- A. The story of Jesus doesn't end with His ascension.
  1. In the Scriptures His story continues in the lives of the disciples.
  2. Today the story goes on through our lives.
- B. The primary assignment of the Church is to lift up Jesus.
  1. We are not a social or political action entity.
  2. There are other groups whose primary cause is to address those issues.
- C. No one else is lifting up Jesus. Therefore, our primary message is to keep the story of Jesus alive.
- D. Read the scripture, Acts 8:1-13.

I. Let's Take a Quick Look at What Happened in the Early Church That Kept the Story of Jesus Alive
- A. The disciples had been filled with the Spirit (chap. 2).
- B. God was doing great things through them (chaps. 3 and 4).
- C. They were holding the things of the world loosely (chap. 5).
- D. They were lifting up Jesus in spite of persecution.
- E. When those in the world do their worst, God does His best.
  1. They crucified Jesus. God raised Him from the dead.
  2. They stoned Stephen. God gave him the face of an angel.

II. In the Momentous Experience of Stephen's Death, a Young Religious Man Saw Jesus
- A. Saul was exposed to Jesus as never before.
  1. Although Saul was not converted at that time, the seeds of his conversion were sown.
  2. There is strong belief that he had observed Jesus but, like most religious rulers, was not ready to follow Him.

    B. The experience of Stephen's death exposed him to Jesus in a special way.
    C. In Acts 8 the entire Church was given the opportunity to lift up Jesus.

III. When Jesus Is Lifted Up, People Respond
    A. With the religious crowd the response may be opposition (v. 3).
    B. How did those who were scattered respond? (v. 4).
    C. Satan must wish he had never started the persecution.
       1. He lost when he crucified Jesus.
       2. He lost again by scattering the believers.
       3. As a result the gospel was spread.
    D. The people of the world are hungry for the truth about God. They are not interested in dull, dry religion. They are interested in Jesus (v. 12).

IV. The Holy Spirit Cannot Be Bought (vv. 14-25)
    A. The power the apostles were demonstrating comes only through the grace of God.
       1. It cannot be earned or bought.
       2. It comes solely as a result of obedience.
    B. The rest of the story is the natural result of turning God loose in our lives.

V. Seeing Jesus Changes Everyone
    A. Philip continued to obey God and lift up Jesus (vv. 26-27).
       1. It seemed like a strange thing to do.
       2. People who are obedient have beautiful experiences.
    B. Philip lifted up Jesus to the Ethiopian eunuch.
    C. The result was that a man far removed from the Church came to Jesus.

Conclusion
    A. Our assignment is to lift up Jesus wherever we may go.
    B. Verse 12 clearly states this assignment and the resulting possibilities for the Church.
    C. As the Church lifts up Jesus, the world will respond.

No Impossible Cases

Acts 9:1-19

Introduction
  A. God's timing is always perfect. The stoning of Stephen as described in chapters 7 and 8 sets the stage for the experiences in chapter 9.
  B. There are three great lessons that are taught in this chapter.
   1. There are no impossible cases with God.
   2. God permits His people to share in what He is doing.
   3. Discipling new converts is exciting.
  C. Read the scripture, Acts 9:1-19.

I. The Church Had Been Pushed Out of Its Comfort Zone
  A. The early Christians were in a situation where they must totally depend on God.
   1. People who depend on Him learn He is worthy of their trust.
   2. Satan can turn up the heat just as he did for the Hebrew children. But God takes care of the details.
  B. Remember these two words: "but God."
   1. Satan stirred the mob into a bloody frenzy as they stoned Stephen, but God opened the heavens.
   2. Satan put Paul and Silas in jail, but God gave them a song.

II. Lesson No. 1: There are no impossible cases (9:1-9)
  A. Meet the man Saul (see Phil. 3).
   1. Pharisee of the Pharisees.
   2. Highly religious.
   3. Zealous in keeping Jewish laws and commandments.
   4. He was a hard case. But there are no impossible cases with God.
  B. The lesson is clear. God takes care of the difficult cases. He did not send Ananias to Paul until He himself had moved on the man.

III. Lesson No. 2: God Uses Obedient People (vv. 10-18)
   A. Ananias was a believer who professed allegiance to Jesus. Read his response to God's call in verse 10: "'Yes, Lord,' he answered."
   B. People in whose lives Jesus is Master are eligible for some wonderful experiences.
      1. Such people have no trouble being obedient.
      2. Their answer is always yes.
      3. Once Ananias was certain of God's instructions, he obeyed (v. 17).
   C. Many religious people live dull, boring, unblessed lives.
      1. Their sins are forgiven, but Jesus is not Master and Lord.
      2. They cheat themselves out of blessings if they never try something that can't be done without God's enablement.
      3. The pure joy of life is realized through obedience to the clear commands of God.

IV. Lesson No. 3: Discipling New Converts Is Exciting (vv. 26-27)
   A. Barnabas (whose name means "the encourager") was a great mentor.
      1. Barnabas stuck to Paul like glue.
      2. He was always helping, encouraging, as he traveled with Paul on his first missionary journey.
      3. Barnabas was willing to do whatever needed to be done.
   B. We wonder what would have happened to Paul's ministry without Barnabas's willingness to disciple and to complete the tasks at hand.

Conclusion
   A. We can expect some hard cases to be broken down and come to know Jesus.
   B. We need some Ananias-type people to come to their side initially.
   C. We then need some Barnabas-type people to rise up to guide these new believers into spiritual maturity.
   D. Remember, there are no impossible cases with God.

The Anatomy of a Happy Home

Acts 10:1-8, 19-25

Introduction
- A. The American home is in desperate need of repair.
  1. Many things have divided the home.
  2. This passage gives us a wonderful model for a Christian home.
- B. There are some basic principles that apply regardless of the size of a family.
  1. When these principles have been established, the results are realized.
  2. The scripture passage for today clearly illustrates the conditions that are required for a healthy, happy home.
  3. Read the scripture, Acts 10:1-8, 19-25.

I. Cornelius Was Head of His Home and Set the Pattern for the Family
- A. As a Gentile, Cornelius was an unlikely candidate. But he is proof that God responds when someone genuinely desires what is best for his or her family.
  1. He was the head of his home and spiritually worthy of that responsibility (v. 2).
  2. The Scriptures indicate that God's first preference is that the father be the head of the home (Noah, Joshua, Joseph).
  3. In some cases women have had to take the lead (e.g., Hannah, Lydia, Eunice).
  4. The key factor is that someone must lead so that the family can follow.
- B. Cornelius was a worthy model as the leader of his family.
  1. He led his family in spiritual matters.
  2. He was a generous man.
  3. His children believed in him because of the way he lived.

    4. He was willing to do whatever was necessary to please God (vv. 4-8).

II. God Was Cornelius's Ally in Reaching His Family
    A. God prepared Peter for his role (vv. 9-19).
    B. Peter responded as obedient followers do (vv. 21-25).
    C. The key to successfully caring for our families' spiritual needs is for the spiritual leader to be obedient to God's plan.
        1. Spiritual leadership implies respect for God and reliance on Him.
        2. Then we must follow His guidance.

III. The Formula for a Happy Home Has Not Changed
    A. Someone must set an example worthy of being followed.
    B. This will require a faithful commitment to spiritual exercises that lift up Jesus. What are those?
        1. Praying regularly
        2. Reading the Word
        3. Giving generously
    C. The spiritual leader of the family must give willing obedience and an immediate response to God's revealed will.
    D. A great biblical example of the influence of a Christian home is Paul's comment to Timothy as recorded in 2 Tim. 1:5. While we know virtually nothing of Timothy's father, we know that his grandmother and mother infected him with a love for God.

Conclusion
    A. If we were to dissect a truly happy home, we would find the following:
        1. Someone in charge who is living a believable Christian life
        2. Someone who is seeking God's highest and best truth
        3. Someone who is pursuing God's will
    B. Happy homes do not come from a secret formula. They are the result of families who want God to have first place in their lives.

The People Called Christians

Acts 11:19-26

Introduction
   A. "Christian" is one of the most abused words in the world.
      1. It is often used to signify people who are non-Jewish, non-Muslim, or nonheathen.
      2. It means infinitely more than any of these implications.
      3. As a church we intend to do everything in our power to bring you into the experience of Christian living.
   B. Many churches have no right to the name Christian.
      1. 60 percent of the ministers in one of the largest denominations state they do not believe in the virgin birth of Jesus Christ.
      2. The Virgin Birth is an absolute essential to being a true believer.
   C. Many non-Christians have concluded that Christianity is no more than a civic club.
      1. They have observed moral weaknesses in some who call themselves Christians.
      2. They have been subjected to a weak belief that is no different from the non-Christian world except in name.
   D. The New Testament church was strong, alive, confident, and different from other religions. Read the scripture, Acts 11:19-26.

I. What Is a Christian?
   A. We begin by eliminating some of the things that are not Christian.
      1. Any organization that denies Jesus' deity, His resurrection, or the validity of the Bible is not Christian.
      2. Just keeping a set of rules is not Christian.
      3. Just being a sincere person is not Christian.
   B. What is a Christian then?

1. Wesley said, "It is one who so believes in Christ that sin has no more dominion over him."
2. It has been defined as one who has a living attachment to the Person, Jesus Christ.
3. It has also been defined as one who seeks first God's kingdom and His righteousness and finds to his or her surprise that everything else in life falls into place.
4. Whatever else we may say, a Christian is a person who believes in and follows Jesus Christ.
5. A Christian is a person who has a positive acceptance of Jesus and an allegiance to Him born of deep love.

II. What Are Christians Like?
   A. Let's look at the people in Antioch who were first called Christians (v. 26).
      1. They were people who had had a personal experience with Jesus.
      2. They were people who displayed the presence of Jesus in their lives (v. 23).
      3. They were people of prayer.
      4. They were people who were interested in others (v. 29).
   B. True Christianity has not changed.
      1. Christians are people who have been exposed to Jesus and subsequently allowed His image to become a part of their lives.
      2. Illustration: Just as Kodak film reveals the image of what it is exposed to, so do we.
      3. Christians are people who have learned to make the most of life in their world.

Conclusion
   A. People called Christians are those who have a personal relationship with Jesus Christ and live like Him.
   B. Because of their lifestyles, they experience the fulfillment of John 10:10 in their lives.

Celebration of Freedom

Acts 12:1-16

Introduction
- A. In chapter 9 we read about Paul's conversion.
    1. He has been released from his imprisonment to the emptiness of his former relationship with God that did not solve his sin problem.
    2. What Paul experienced before his conversion was a diplomatic relationship with God.
    3. What Paul enjoyed after his conversion was a warm, loving relationship with his Father.
- B. In chapter 10 the message of Jesus had also spread into the Gentile community.
    1. Cornelius, a Roman centurion, brought his family into the Christian fold.
    2. The gospel was spreading.
- C. In chapter 11 the message of Jesus had spread to Antioch.
    1. It was in Antioch that believers were first called Christians.
    2. They were true believers.
- D. In chapter 12 the non-Christian world was deeply disturbed and determined to do everything possible to halt the spread of the gospel.
    1. When things are going well in the Church—look out! Satan will find a way to create problems.
    2. Read the scripture, Acts 12:1-16.

I. Peter Has Been Thrown into Jail (vv. 3-4)
- A. Herod has killed James, the brother of John (v. 2).
    1. As politicians do, to please the people (the Jews), he jailed Peter (v. 3).
    2. He made sure Peter could not escape (v. 4).
- B. Herod underestimated the power of a praying church (v. 5).

II. Peter Is Dramatically Released (vv. 6-7)
- A. God responded to the prayers of His people (v. 6).

1. Never forget this: God is in charge and always has the final say.
2. Satan cannot do what God cannot undo.
   B. According to verse 6, Satan appeared to be totally in charge of the situation.
      1. This was not the first time he lost the battle.
      2. Remember the three Hebrew young men in Dan. 3.
      3. Remember Daniel's experience in the lions' den (Dan. 6).
   C. God miraculously released Peter (Acts 12:7-10).
      1. Peter's chains fell off.
      2. The prison door opened.
      3. He walked out of jail as a free man.
      4. He went to the house where God's people were gathered.
   D. Peter's release brought great joy to the Church.
      1. At first, they had trouble believing he was free (vv. 13-15).
      2. Experiences such as these release the Church from fear of the enemy.

III. We Can Celebrate This Same Freedom in Our Hearts and Lives Today

   A. Satan says, "I have You under my control." God responds, "Oh, no you don't!"
   B. We have received great news! The prison door of slavery to sin is open, and we don't have to stay there!
      1. Those of us who respond to God's guidance enjoy great freedom.
      2. We may feel as Peter did in verse 9, but we can also ultimately feel as Peter did in verse 11.

Conclusion

   A. What the committed, obedient people of God enjoy seems like a dream.
      1. It isn't. This life is for real.
      2. We may not understand it, but we enjoy what God has done for us.
   B. If Satan still has you imprisoned in a sinful life, God offers you freedom.
   C. The choice is up to you.

The Key to Great Joy

Acts 13:1-12, 44-52

Introduction
A. Between the opening and closing of this chapter the key to one of life's greatest treasures is clearly presented.
   1. That treasure is a life of overflowing joy.
   2. The key to a joy-filled life is obedience to the clearly revealed will of God.
B. Many Christians live beneath their privilege because they fail to be totally obedient to God's will.
C. In our scripture today the Church is marching on. As a result of its obedience, wonderful things are happening.
D. Read the scripture, Acts 13:1-12, 44-52.

I. Paul and Barnabas Found the Treasure by Being Obedient to God's Will (vv. 2-3)
A. They found this treasure by following the clearly revealed will of God rather than going along with what most of the Church was doing.
   1. They left the traditions of the day that presumed God only loved certain people.
   2. The traditions of the day are demonstrated in verses 42-45.
B. Paul and Barnabas obeyed even though they may not have understood.
C. God promises great blessings to those who obey Him (Isa. 1:19).
   1. The reason some people struggle is because they argue with God.
   2. They fail to relax in His will.
D. The Scriptures give numerous illustrations of the wisdom of obedience.
   1. In Josh. 3 the only way across the raging river to the Promised Land was through obedience.
   2. God does not explain His actions. He says, "Trust Me."

II. This Chapter Is a Call for the Church to Follow God's Leading

A. Paul reminded them of the price of disobedience (Acts 13:16-22).
   1. The Israelites wandered in the wilderness because they failed to trust God (vv. 17-18).
   2. God removed Saul as king because he failed to trust Him (v. 22).
   3. We cannot expect God to treat us any differently today if we disobey Him.
B. All through the earlier chapters of Acts, the obedient disciples used their resources for God's glory. Thus we read that they experienced great joy and blessings.
   1. Look at chapters 2, 4, and 11.
   2. It is greatly rewarding to use our material blessings for God's glory.
C. It is easy to be obedient if we remember our Source of blessings.
   1. God is the Giver of all of our resources.
   2. If I give away all that I have in obedience to Him, He will replace it many times over.

Conclusion

A. God takes pleasure in people who put Him first.
B. We believe that happy fathers have happy children. This applies to God's children as well.
C. If you want to experience the joy of verse 13:52, practice obedience as it is laid out in the early part of this chapter.

The Good News Passed On

Acts 13:32-48

Introduction
   A. Paul was on his first journey as a missionary.
      1. He and Barnabas had been encouraged by the church at Antioch to go (vv. 1-3).
      2. They had some interesting experiences.
         a. A false prophet was blinded (vv. 6-11).
         b. John Mark got homesick and returned to Jerusalem.
   B. They had an interesting experience in the synagogue at Pisidian Antioch.
      1. The custom was to open the floor for testimonies (v. 15).
      2. Paul took advantage of that opportunity to preach the message of Jesus to them.
      3. It is this message that we are looking at today.
      4. Read the scripture, Acts 13:32-48.

I. The Promise Fulfilled (vv. 32-33)
   A. The people of Israel had looked for a deliverer, the Messiah.
      1. They interpreted that promise in a political sense.
      2. God had a better plan in mind.
      3. There is a deliverance that is greater than the physical, political one.
      4. Paul was telling them that the promise for deliverance has already been fulfilled.
   B. We can experience the fulfillment of the promise in our lives today.
      1. "I have Good News for you" (see v. 32).
      2. Today we have the freedom of knowing in our lives what others are still seeking.

II. The Assurance of forgiveness (vv. 38-39)
   A. There is forgiveness for all of our sins.

        1. Any sin—all sin.
        2. No sin in excluded, and that is good news.
        3. Since there is no new sin, the grace of Jesus Christ is still sufficient today.
   B. This forgiveness is not difficult to experience (v. 39).
        1. The forgiveness of our sins is the central theme of the Bible.
        2. Keeping the law does not make us righteous (v. 39).
        3. Salvation is found through simply coming to Jesus Christ.

III. The Warning Given (vv. 40-41)
   A. No one is forced to believe.
        1. There are some people who simply will not believe even though the evidence is overwhelming (v. 41).
        2. No one can be forced to believe in Jesus against his or her will.
   B. The options are very clear.
        1. Those who reject Jesus do not know the realization of the promise of forgiveness.
        2. Those who hear and respond will know the fulfillment of the promise.
        3. Illustrate by comparing the promise of Canaan. Ten spies resisted; two believed and experienced the joy (see Num. 13).

Conclusion
   A. The Jews, being jealous, were intrigued but did not repent (Acts 13:46).
   B. Paul passed the Good News on to the Gentiles (v. 47).
   C. The Gentiles heard, responded, and found forgiveness and great joy.
   D. The Good News is passed on to us today. What will you do with it?

The Place of the Church in Today's World

Acts 15:1-21

Introduction
- A. The Church was growing, and growing churches usually have problems.
  1. Sometimes the problems come from outside of the Church (see chaps. 8 and 12).
  2. Sometimes the problems come from internal sources and are the result of honest differences of opinion.
- B. In chapter 15 we find some sharp disagreements within the Church.
  1. Paul and Barnabas had been on their first missionary journey.
  2. While they gave a good report from their journey, some of the elders were not pleased.
  3. Read the scripture, Acts 15:1-21.

I. Opinions Vary About How the Church Is to Operate (vv. 1-2)
- A. The question of the observance of Jewish law by Gentiles in order to be Christians is the issue.
  1. Do Jews have exclusive rights to God's love?
  2. Is salvation found through the Jews alone?
- B. This issue raises pertinent questions for the Church today.
  1. What is the role of the Church?
  2. Why must we be part of a church?
  3. What are the standards by which we are measured?

II. The Bible Clearly Establishes an Organized Church
- A. There are those who do not believe in the necessity of an organized church.
  1. Most people who fall into this category simply do not want any strings of authority attached to their lives.
  2. They usually end up living chaotic lives.
- B. It is true. The Church does not save us. We are saved through Jesus alone.

1. We understand the strength that comes from unity.
2. Success is multiplied as we work together.

III. The New Testament Church Was Organized (vv. 4-6)
A. The biblical picture of the Church is clearly a structured one.
   1. Look at chapter 6.
   2. In this passage we read that there were apostles and elders.
   3. In Paul's writings in 1 Tim. 3 he outlines the responsibilities of overseers and deacons.
B. Why was the Church organized?
   1. It was organized because we worship an orderly God.
   2. The universe is organized so that it will function at its best.
C. Everyone needs some kind of an accountability program.
   1. We need someone to look to as a higher authority.
   2. Those who have no commitment to authority will self-destruct.

IV. The Bible Clearly Raises Some Standards of Conduct (vv. 15-29)
A. These are clearly biblical guidelines of conduct.
B. The Ten Commandments are standards of conduct that God expects of us.
C. While standards of conduct can be like a fence, they can also provide great freedom within those boundaries.
D. Thus there is no question about what God expects from us.

Conclusion
A. The role of the Church is to tell us about God's love as clearly revealed through Jesus.
B. The Church challenges us to live for the One who died for us.
C. The role of the Church is not encouraged to see what we can do and still go to heaven. Rather, it is to see how brightly we can shine as we radiate the power and love of God to a lost world.

Lessons from Philippi

Acts 16:16-40

Introduction
A. People who learn from the successes and failures of others are destined for a life filled with positive experiences.
  1. They avoid many of the mistakes of others.
  2. They enjoy many of the successes of others.
  3. A wise person looks at the life of someone else and learns by letting the Holy Spirit speak through his or her observations.
B. This is what we are doing in this message—learning lessons from Paul's and Silas's experiences in Philippi.
  1. On Paul's second missionary journey he and Silas were led of God to cross the Aegean into Macedonia to share the message of Jesus.
  2. We can learn four great lessons from their experiences in Philippi.
  3. Read the scripture, Acts 16:16-40.

I. Lesson No. 1: The non-Christian world has a set of faulty values (vv. 16-24).
A. We read about a young, demon-possessed girl who was being used by some men for their own profit.
  1. They made money from her psychic powers.
  2. She was telling the truth (v. 17).
  3. Paul commanded the evil spirit to come out of her (v. 19).
B. Her owners became upset over their loss of income.
  1. They did not value the girl.
  2. The non-Christian world uses and abuses humanity.
C. Why is our world in such a mess?
  1. The route of sin is always degrading.
  2. Our society is more pleasure oriented than people oriented.
D. The Church believes in improving people, not abusing people.

II. Lesson No. 2: God Delivers His People from Bondage (vv. 25-26)
   A. This is a powerful lesson for us to learn.
      1. Paul and Silas were jailed unjustly.
      2. Their attitude is amazing (v. 25).
   B. Faithful people find satisfaction in being found worthy to suffer for Jesus.
      1. Remember 5:41—Peter and the apostles were overjoyed.
      2. In this passage Paul and Silas discover this same joy.
   C. The lesson is clear. God is in charge. We have no reason to fear.
      1. If the Church stays focused on the grace and power of God, the outside world will be more interested in coming to know Him.
      2. We are not poor, weak, mistreated worms in the dust.
      3. We are children of the King of the universe.
      4. Satan cannot put us where the grace of God cannot reach us.

III. Lesson No. 3: The Road to Really Living Is Found in Jesus Christ (16:27-31)
   A. The jailer saw something he wanted.
   B. Christians demonstrate a joy regardless of life's situation that is attractive to the outside world.
   C. Christians manifest joy along with a healthy state of emotional well-being.

IV. Lesson No. 4: God Is a Great Compensator (vv. 32-34)
   A. Because of their attitudes, Paul and Silas were richly rewarded by God.
   B. The greatest reward of all was realizing the conversion of the jailer and his family.
   C. God has a wonderful way of compensating His people for any problem we endure while serving Him.

Conclusion
   A. May God help us learn from these four great lessons from Philippi.
   B. These lessons will change our lives forever.

Christianity Simplified

Acts 16:25-34

Introduction
- A. Paul and Silas found a good way to stir up trouble.
  1. Get in the way of the sinner's pocketbook.
  2. The girl's owners were upset when their finances were disrupted.
  3. They had Paul and Silas put into prison (vv. 19-23).
- B. There is a lesson for Christians in this event.
  1. When the world is convicted by our lives, it will react against us.
  2. When we infringe on Satan's territory, he always fights back.
- C. If Christians sustain a right attitude, the results are wonderful. Read the scripture, Acts 16:25-34.

I. Paul and Silas Had a Right to Complain
- A. They were innocent and did not deserve the treatment they received.
  1. They had restored self-respect and value to a human being.
  2. For this they were stripped and beaten (vv. 22-23).
  3. Their persecutors thought they had defeated them (v. 24).
  4. The jailer had to listen to their praises.
- B. We have no right to complain.
  1. God never promised an easy road. He promised grace for each day.
  2. When our attitudes are right, our lives manifest Christ's love.
- C. Paul and Silas had a right to complain but chose to testify instead.

II. Everyone Had a Right to Be Afraid (vv. 26-28)
- A. God came to the prison at midnight.
  1. They were sitting in heavenly places spiritually (v. 25).

      2. God will not stand idly by while His innocent children are mistreated.
      3. All of the prisoners were freed. When God's faithful ones are blessed, the blessings spill over.
      4. The jailer was in despair and ready to commit suicide.
  B. This hopeless condition eventually comes to all sinners when the foundations of their lives crumbles beneath them.

III. The Jailer Asked a Simple Question (v. 30)
  A. He had observed Paul and Silas's reaction to a hopeless situation.
      1. Their joy and confidence under fire convinced him that they had something he wanted
      2. He asked, "What must I do to be saved?" (v. 30).
  B. Multitudes of others have asked this same simple question.
      1. The rich young ruler asked (Mark 10:17-31).
      2. The Ethiopian eunuch asked (Acts 8:26-40).

IV. Paul Gave Him a Simple Answer (16:31)
  A. Notice how simple the answer is.
      1. "Just believe in the Lord Jesus Christ."
      2. "Turn from sin to the Savior."
  B. It is still that simple today.
      1. Accept Jesus Christ as your Savior.
      2. When a person truly wants to be saved, it is easy to do so.

V. The Result of the Jailer's Action
  A. There was great rejoicing (v. 34).
      1. His life was totally transformed.
      2. Note the jailer's actions in verses 33-34.
  B. Joy still comes to believers.

Conclusion
  A. The question today remains, "What must I do to be saved?"
  B. Confess your sins and invite Jesus to come into your heart.

A Second Work of Grace

Acts 19:1-7

Introduction
A. The people in this scripture passage were genuine converts. It is clear they believed in the Lord Jesus Christ.
B. Paul wanted them to experience all God had for them.
   1. Many believers stop short of their full Christian potential.
   2. Paul wanted this crowd to have all God had promised.
   3. This experience would be the key to their survival in the midst of a morally bankrupt society.
C. Read the scripture, Acts 19:1-7.

I. The Question Paul Asked Is a Personal One (v. 2)
A. Note the personal pronoun "you."
   1. It is essential to have a personal experience with the Holy Spirit.
   2. They could not rely on the experiences of earlier believers.
   3. No one else can make your consecration for you.
   4. No one else can have the faith necessary for your experience.
B. It is a pointed question.
   1. It is clear to whom Paul is addressing this question.
   2. Some people try to evade the personal encounter required.
C. The matter at hand requires surrendering the control of our lives to God. In simple form, this is a total personal commitment.

II. The Question Paul Asked Is a Searching One (v. 2)
A. "Did you accept God's great gift to you?"
   1. This is the will of God for our lives (1 Thess. 4:3).
   2. A gift does not become ours until we receive and take ownership of it.

    B. Ownership necessitates a willful acceptance.
       1. It is a voluntary act on the part of the receiver.
       2. Illustration: No one had forced the early believers to tarry in the Upper Room.
       3. No one can pressure you to come into your Upper Room experience.

III. The Question Involves the Holy Spirit

    A. Many would believe that this is synonymous with the experience of entire sanctification.*
       1. In 1:8 we read that they would receive power from the Holy Spirit.
       2. It is the Holy Spirit that "sets us apart for sacred use."
    B. Understanding the Holy Spirit.
       1. He is the empowering arm of God.
       2. He is the Third Person of the Trinity.

IV. The Question Implies a Previous Experience with God

    A. Paul inferred that they had believed on the Lord Jesus Christ.
       1. Why does this not happen at the same time?
       2. The nature of each work is different.
       3. When we first come to Christ, we ask for forgiveness.
       4. In this experience we consecrate our forgiven lives to Him.
    B. When Paul prayed for these Christians, the Holy Spirit came upon them.
       1. Note 19:6.
       2. Illustration: A similar experience happened in the home of Cornelius as recorded in 10:44.

Conclusion

    A. Have you received the Holy Spirit since you believed?
    B. Consecrate your forgiven life to Him.
    C. Enjoy the baptism of the Holy Spirit, and you, too, can survive in the midst of a morally bankrupt society.

---

*Most modern translations render the question in verse 2 as, "Did you receive the Holy Spirit when you believed?" The Greek construction for "believed" is a participle that can be translated "after (or since) you believed."

The Great Change That Jesus Brings

Acts 26:1-19

Introduction
- A. There are many areas where we can get help to improve our lives.
    1. A good friend can give a lift when we are discouraged.
    2. A banker can give financial help.
    3. A counselor can help overcome depression.
    4. A physician can help us when we are sick.
    5. All of these are good and help the quality of our lives. But they cannot supply our deepest need—forgiveness from our sins.
    6. Only Jesus can make the change we need.
- B. Paul is the perfect illustration of a personal encounter with Jesus.
    1. Paul's testimony is a revelation of this great truth.
    2. Read the scripture, Acts 26:1-19.

I. Paul Had Everything Most People Consider Important

- A. His living conditions were equal to what most people desire.
    1. He was from a wealthy family.
    2. He was highly educated.
    3. His position as a Pharisee gave him prestige.
    4. None of these conditions satisfied the deepest need of his life.
- B. Paul needed something to satisfy the internal emptiness he experienced.
    1. Some think the attack he unleashed on the Christian Church was a cover-up for his misery.
    2. He had seen the reflection of Jesus in Stephen's life and death and could not get away from that.
    3. Fortunately, God loves miserable people too.

II. God Intervened with a Special Encounter (vv. 12-14)
   A. God never gives up on anyone. He reaches out to every human being.
   B. In the Old Testament God is constantly reaching out to Israel. The prophet Hosea modeled God's unfailing love to Israel.
   C. In the New Testament Jesus reaches out to the undesirable.
      1. The woman at the well (John 4)
      2. The thief on the cross (Luke 23)
      3. A tax collector (Matt. 9:9)
   D. Jesus planned a special encounter for Paul.
      1. He has planned a similar individual encounter for each one of us.
      2. He wants to make the change in each of our lives as He did for Paul.
      3. This divine-human encounter will change our lives forever.

III. The Results of the Change
   A. Paul's life was transformed
      1. From anger and hatred to peace and love
      2. From searching and frustration to enjoyment and fulfillment
   B. As a result Paul was able to speak with confidence about his relationship with God (Acts 26:22).
   C. The change in our lives can be just as great.
      1. Things that previously ruled our lives become insignificant.
      2. The encounter with Jesus brings the qualities of life that matter most.

Conclusion
   A. Paul's testimony in the closing hours of his life is that of a man who is satisfied with his life (2 Tim. 4:6-18).
   B. We, too, can experience such a change in our lives today.

Lessons from Paul

Acts 26:1-19

Introduction
A. The subject of today's message is one of the most conspicuous people in human history.
  1. It has been said that other than the life of Jesus no other life is more worthy of study than that of Paul.
  2. Paul's conversion proved that the power of Christianity could overcome the strongest of prejudices.
  3. The leading topic of Paul's thinking was to explain in an understandable way why Jesus died.
  4. Paul wrote 13 letters that clearly show his focus on the plan of redemption as revealed in Jesus.
  5. Because of Paul's obsession, the message of Jesus Christ went forth through him to evangelize the world.
B. This powerful person has many lessons to teach us.
  1. Paul's testimony before King Agrippa is a clear witness from one who knows what Jesus did for him.
  2. Read the scripture, Acts 26:1-19.

I. Lesson No. 1: There Is More to Pleasing God than Being Religious
A. Paul was a very religious man (vv. 4-5).
  1. He had been trained to be a rabbi and knew the Old Testament well.
  2. In Phil. 3:4-6 Paul repeats his religious qualifications.
  3. Paul's experience was in his mind. God wants also to make it a matter of heart.
B. Paul's experience reminds us of the rich young ruler's encounter with Jesus (Matt. 19).
  1. That young man also had a religion of the mind that never penetrated his heart.
  2. He went away defeated.
C. It still takes more than religion to please God.

II. Lesson No. 2: God Is No Respecter of Persons
   A. While Paul was a religious man, he was a mean man.
      1. Note Acts 26:9-12.
      2. When Ananias was told to see Paul, he was shocked (9:13-14).
      3. Note Paul's testimony in 1 Tim. 1:15.
   B. The story of the Bible is that Jesus loves all of us—sinners as well.
      1. Zacchaeus (Luke 19)
      2. The woman at the well (John 4)
      3. The thief on the cross (Luke 23)
   C. Today we can still say that there are no unlovable people in Jesus' eyes.

III. Lesson No. 3: When God Has His Way, Lives Are Dramatically Changed
   A. Paul's conversion resulted in a miraculous change (Acts 26:14-18).
   B. It has always been this way (Luke 8).
      1. The Gerasene demoniac was radically transformed (v. 26).
      2. Mary Magdalene was totally changed (vv. 1-2).
   C. Jesus still changes lives today.

Conclusion
   A. How are these lessons fulfilled in one's life? Look at Acts 26:19.
   B. God can still change anyone's life today.
      1. You cannot be good enough.
      2. No one is too far gone.

Four Anchors

Acts 27:13-36

Introduction
A. Life is a conglomeration of experiences—some good, some bad.
   1. It is a wholesome thing when we realize that human beings do not live on an even plane.
   2. We have a tendency to rejoice when all is well and to fall apart when it is not.
B. Three simple truths will help us face difficult times.
   1. Storms do not mean divine disapproval.
   2. To be in a stormy moment is not sinful.
   3. There are anchors to hold us steady in times of stress.
C. Paul's experience in Acts 27 supports these truths.
   1. Read the scripture, verses 13-36.
   2. Paul had four anchors that held him steady just as the four anchors on the ship.

I. He Had a Firm Faith in God (v. 23)
A. Paul was fully persuaded about the reality of God.
   1. This is absolutely essential to sustaining a steady soul.
   2. This assurance removes all doubts about the outcome.
B. To believe in the reality of God means that life and all that surround it are under His control.
   1. While God does not send everything, He has the final say in every situation.
   2. Illustrate with the experience of the Hebrew children in Dan. 3.

II. He Had Faith in God's Word (Acts 27:25)
A. God means what He says.
   1. The physical surroundings were not encouraging.
   2. Paul's faith was not limited to what he could see.
   3. God said "Do not be afraid," and Paul wasn't (v. 24).

B. We tend to give great lip service to God's Word.
      1. Sometimes we have difficulty believing when we have problems.
      2. Those who do believe live stable Christian lives.

III. He Had a Firm Personal Relationship with God (v. 23)
   A. Paul had built a mature relationship with God.
      1. It was not just that he knew about God—He knew God.
      2. The questions were settled in his life and mind.
   B. There is no substitute for this anchor.
      1. To know about God is not enough.
      2. Intellect without relationship can be frustrating.

IV. He Was Abandoned to His Faith in God (vv. 30-32)
   A. Paul was totally committed to God's guidance.
      1. He did not have to understand what God was doing to trust Him.
      2. Paul accepted that God works in mysterious ways.
   B. We must come to the place where we don't have to have all of the answers.
      1. This shifts the responsibility for the outcome to God.
      2. If we hold back, the responsibility will be ours.
      3. Abandoning ourselves to God gives us a great anchor.

Conclusion
   A. Life will not be easy. It can be victorious with these four anchors.
      1. Faith in God
      2. Faith in His Word
      3. A firm personal relationship with God
      4. A Commitment to His way
   B. With these anchors we will not only survive, as Paul did, but also take others with us.

Finding a Place of Safety

Acts 27:33-44

Introduction
   A. Paul's experience on his way to Rome speaks to a great truth in Christian living. Read Acts 27:33-44.
      1. Paul was a faithful man of God (chap. 26).
      2. He was in a life-threatening situation (27:17-20)
      3. He was in trouble because of circumstances beyond his control (vv. 9-11).
      4. Paul was able to stay calm when others were in distress (vv. 19-25).
      5. Paul's faith was vindicated (vv. 41-44).
   B. We must make sure we are prepared for the severe storms that will come into our lives today.
      1. Paul had come to a great attitude about life (Phil. 4:11-13).
      2. He had found the secret of surviving whatever came his way.

I. The Question of Storms in Our Lives
   A. Do believers suffer?
      1. Absolutely. It is natural for humankind to experience difficulties.
      2. The idea that pain and hurting is a result of sin is not scriptural.
      3. Look at Job, Daniel, and Paul.
      4. Jesus himself was subjected to many of the same pressures we experience.
   B. At times in our desire to understand trials we make the assumption that we deserve what we get.
      1. Did Jesus?
      2. Did Paul?
      3. Sometimes we do. But many times we do not.

II. What Should We Do When Stormy Situations Come?
A. We must find a place of safety.
1. Illustration: When tornadoes head our way, we head for shelter.
2. Illustration: When severe snowstorms are coming, we head for safety.
B. What about the other storms of life?
1. When sorrow, financial reversals, and other problems come, we seek a place of safety.
2. Sometimes the greatest miracle is not the removal of the storm but in having the ability to survive it.
3. Survivors learn how to handle subsequent situations.
4. This was Paul's pathway to success (2 Tim. 4:6-8).

III. How Do We Build a Spiritual Storm Shelter?
A. We must begin with a strong relationship with Jesus Christ.
1. A personal encounter with Jesus
2. Absolute faith in His guidance
3. An obedient life surrendered to His will
B. Many people wait until there is a cloud on the horizon to start building their shelter.
1. The Bible makes it very clear that all of us will have storms (Matt. 7:24).
2. Knowing this, why do we wait to begin to make preparations for the inevitable?
3. Why not make sure that we are indestructible? (2 Cor. 1:8-11; 4:7-18).

Conclusion
A. Have you started building your storm shelter?
B. You may need it sooner than you think.

The Life That Really Matters

Galatians 2:11-20

Introduction
- A. Let's look at the background of this text.
  1. Two good men had an encounter in Antioch (vv. 11-12). One of them had found a freedom that the other one did not enjoy.
  2. Peter was trying to live in two worlds—the world of grace in Jesus and the world of the Jewish law.
  3. Paul was a one-dimensional man—grace in Jesus alone (v. 19).
  4. Paul gives the key to the life that really matters.
  5. Read the scripture, Gal. 2:11-20.
- B. Everyone has a life to live.
  1. It can be meaningful and fruitful.
  2. It can be a life of constantly recycling meaningless experiences.

I. The Life That Matters Is Realized Through Making Three Dramatic Decisions
- A. Decision one is acknowledging that salvation comes through Jesus alone.
  1. No one can save himself or herself.
  2. Rituals and ceremonies cannot save us.
  3. As Peter said in Acts 4:12, we recognize that our only hope is found in Jesus.
- B. Decision two recognizes the true nature of sin.
  1. Sin is totally disruptive to sustaining a right relationship with God.
  2. God never has and never will fellowship with sin.
  3. Sin is like an insidious disease that sometimes rages, sometimes subsides, but always leads to death.
- C. Decision three is acknowledging that no one ever reaches his or her greatest potential without a total commitment to Jesus Christ.
  1. Those who truly serve Him have no regrets.

2. Outside of this commitment, Paul would not have ever known the great life that he experienced.

II. Look at the Life That Paul Lived (Gal. 2:20)
   A. It was a victorious life.
      1. Although Paul had problems, he was an overcomer (Phil. 4:12-13).
      2. The person who lives a life that truly matters will reflect that same spirit of confidence.
   B. It was a life that was powerful in impact.
      1. Paul made an impact on the world that has reverberated through 2000 years.
      2. He was the author of 13 books of the New Testament.
      3. We may never write a book, but we can make a difference in our world.
   C. Paul's life reflected an adventuresome spirit.
      1. He was not afraid to go into new territory.
      2. There is always a sense of adventure when we are delivered from ourselves.
   D. It was a life that was fruitful in outcome.
      1. Who could have possibly made a greater impact than Paul?
      2. There is a rich sense of satisfaction that comes from knowing that God has used us to help someone else.

Conclusion
   A. No one can enjoy living in two worlds as Peter tried to do.
   B. The way to experience the life that really matters is to follow Paul's example of total surrender to Jesus Christ.

A Choice to Make

Galatians 5:16-26

Introduction
   A. Our lesson for this message looks at one of the simplest truths of life that is a real problem for some people.
      1. The lesson is expressed in several different passages, including Gal. 6:7 and Matt. 7:17-20.
      2. The lesson is very clear. The life we live is a direct result of the choices we make.
      3. Every choice in life has its price.
   B. Paul is trying to open the Galatians' eyes to the choice that is before them.
      1. He assumes that once they clearly see the options, they will make the right choice.
      2. Read the scripture, Gal. 5:16-26.

I. Look at the War Within (v. 17)
   A. Notice that we do not have to teach wrongdoing. It is the direct result of the sinful nature.
      1. Sin fosters a degrading nature.
      2. This explains how sinful people can be so mean to others.
      3. While we do not like the ugliness of sin, once we cast our vote with the enemy, we lose control.
   B. The Holy Spirit leads in a path contradictory to the drives of the flesh.
      1. Verse 17 from *The Living Bible* reads, "The good things we want to do when the Spirit has his way with us are just the opposite of our natural desires."
      2. In verse 18, we read that those who are led by the Spirit are not in bondage to anything.
      3. Those who submit to the flesh become its slaves.

II. Look at the Works of the Flesh (vv. 19-21)
   A. These will be present in your life if you choose the path of the flesh.

        1. We do not choose which ones we support.
        2. The works of the flesh fall into four groups.
   B. Group one deals with sexual sins (v. 19).
        1. The moral climate of Paul's world was sexually explicit.
        2. The moral climate of our world today is sexually explicit.
        3. Sex is the easiest idol for the enemy to use to draw humankind away from God.
   C. Group two deals with false worship (v. 20).
        1. Idolatry—simply letting anything become more important than God.
        2. Sorcery—the use of anything other than the Bible to aid the spirit life.
   D. Group three deals with the social vices (vv. 20*b*-21).
   E. Group four deals with vices of the appetites (v. 21).
        1. Drunkenness
        2. Wild parties
   F. We want to pick our sins, but life doesn't work like that.
        1. In verse 21 note the words "and the like."
        2. This is a phrase that leaves the list open-ended to whatever comes along.

III. The Fruit of the Spirit (vv. 22-23)
   A. It is important to note that it is "fruit" (singular). Those who have one experience all of them.
   B. No one questions that the world would be a better place if the fruit of the Spirit were pursued rather than the works of the flesh.

Conclusion
   A. Every one of us has a choice to make regarding which lifestyle he or she will support.
   B. The choice before us is very clear.
   C. According to verse 21*b*, those who pursue the flesh will not inherit the kingdom of God.

A Magnificent Obsession

Philippians 1:21; 3:7-11

Introduction
- A. What is an obsession?
    1. It is a total occupation with something until nothing else matters.
    2. It is the pursuit of an idea, purpose, or goal that takes precedence over everything else.
    3. To be magnificent it has to be an idea, thought, or ambition of great beauty or worth.
- B. It is easy to see that Paul's testimony from a Roman jail was an admission of an obsession.
    1. Paul is saying, "Life and Jesus Christ are inseparable to me."
    2. Moffatt translates Phil. 1:21, "Life means Christ to me."
    3. Christ is not something. He is everything.
    4. Read the scripture, Phil. 1:21; 3:7-11.

I. Life Means Different Things to Different People
- A. Some people are obsessed with earthly pleasure. Illustration: Many sports figures become so obsessed with their performance that they train constantly.
- B. Some people are obsessed with earthly possessions. Illustration: Some people have amassed great wealth at the expense of their families.
- C. These things create boundaries to life's joy.
    1. When these temporal things come to an end, so does the joy of life.
    2. This condition puts limits on when, where, and how we enjoy life.
- D. To Paul, life meant Jesus Christ.
    1. Jesus is life without limits.
    2. He is everywhere.
    3. He never comes to an end (Heb. 13:8).

    E. To truly experience Jesus and all He has for us, He must be our obsession.
       1. Jesus becomes as natural to our lives as breathing.
       2. He takes the struggles of life away.

II. Paul Was Obsessed with Jesus

    A. Paul had been obsessed with the legalism of the Pharisees.
       1. This obsession made him hard, critical, and mean.
       2. Whatever has major priority in our lives determines our attitude toward everything else.
    B. Paul met Jesus in a face-to-face encounter.
       1. He lost sight of a lesser goal and gained the greater one (Phil. 3:7).
       2. Jesus makes everything else cheap and unimportant (v. 8).
    C. Paul became obsessed with Jesus.
       1. Paul talked about Jesus everywhere he went.
       2. He burned out his life running around the world to share the gospel of Jesus Christ.
       3. Illustration: Paul's obsession with Jesus inspired him to make the missionary journeys recorded in the Book of Acts.
       4. Everything Paul did had one goal, and that was to lift up Jesus Christ.
       5. Paul's activity was not a meaningless effort from the head. It was the burning ambition of his heart.

Conclusion

    A. We need to be people like Paul—obsessed by a desire to experience more and more of Jesus.
    B. The more we become obsessed with Jesus, the more we share Paul's testimony in Phil. 3:7-11.

Press On

Philippians 3:7-21

Introduction
A. The Philippian letter is Paul's testimony to the church at Philippi.
   1. It gives great insights into his personal life.
   2. Paul uses a personal pronoun over 100 times in this short Epistle.
   3. Paul is in the worst physical condition but is in the best spiritual condition.
   4. This letter was written from a Roman jail following the perilous voyage mentioned in Acts 27.
   5. Still, Paul is confident, positive, and committed to Jesus.
B. We can learn some things from Paul, who demonstrated such a great attitude toward life regardless of his circumstances.
   1. Paul tells us how to live confidently in the face of the worst of storms.
   2. He tells us how to keep our lives fresh and meaningful.
   3. Many people do not enjoy life because they have "stale" commitments.
   4. When a person feels that he or she has arrived, that person is in danger of becoming stale.
   5. Read the scripture, Phil. 3:7-21.

I. Listen to Paul's Testimony of Commitment (vv. 12-14)
A. Remember Paul's spiritual journey.
   1. Converted on the road to Damascus (see Acts 9).
   2. Baptized and filled with the Spirit at Ananias's house (v. 17).
   3. Obedient to the call of God (26:19).
   4. Poured himself into the work of God.
   5. Still he confesses, "I have not arrived" (see Phil. 3:12).
B. To have "arrived" means we have gone over the crest of the hill.

1. We are either going up, have reached the top, or are going down.
2. This is why it is so important that we understand "the need to strive for more of Jesus" attitude.
3. To maintain this commitment does not detract from our confidence.
C. This attitude does not reflect on being "saved by grace."
1. We are saved by grace. We grow spiritually by works.
2. Those who do not grow spiritually begin to die spiritually.

II. Look at the Practical Considerations of This Commitment

A. We must forget what is behind (v. 13).
1. Paul has taken note of his journey to this point (vv. 4-7).
2. He refuses to live in the past.
3. We do well to reflect on our journey, but we must always realize that there is a greater journey ahead of us.
B. We must reach forward (vv. 13-14).
1. This expression clearly presents the picture of one who is committed to winning.
2. It is not enough just to start or run a race. We must reach the finish line triumphantly.

Conclusion

A. What would happen if every believer in this congregation decided to press on in his or her relationship with Jesus?
B. Paul found the life of inner satisfaction that we all seek.
C. This passage tells us how he achieved that satisfaction.
D. Join me in following Paul's example as expressed in verses 15-17.

Faith in Daily Living

James 2:14-26

Introduction
A. There seems to be something mystical about faith.
   1. Heb. 11:1 states that "faith is being sure of what we hope for and certain of what we do not see."
   2. While this is the biblical definition of faith, it does not help us to understand totally how faith applies to our daily lives.
   3. We will combine today's text with Heb. 11 to get a practical understanding.
B. For our purposes we will define faith as an outward action that demonstrates an inward belief.
   1. Faith is the manifestation of what we say we believe in our physical lives.
   2. Read the scripture, James 2:14-26.

I. A Brief Look at Heb. 11
A. Examine Noah's faith.
   1. He believed that God was speaking to him.
   2. He confirmed it by building the ark.
B. Look at Abraham's faith.
   1. He believed that God was guiding his life.
   2. He confirmed it by leaving home at age 75 and later by being willing to offer Isaac as a sacrifice.
C. Look at Moses' faith.
   1. He believed that God spoke to him in the desert.
   2. He confirmed it when he confronted Pharaoh.
D. Our belief becomes faith when we act upon it. Faith is mixing the energy of our lives with what we say we believe.

II. A Brief Look at Our Selected Passage in James 2
A. James is recognized as the book of practical experience.
   1. Paul's writings are theological in nature.
   2. John's writings emphasize the love of God.

3. James's writings help us with practical living.
   B. James makes the point very clear that faith does not exist unless it is physically demonstrated. Note verses 14, 17, 18, 21, and 26.

III. Faith in Our Daily Lives
   A. In order to please God we must get beyond words.
   B. How do we demonstrate faith in practical living?
      1. We can do this by being faithful in church attendance.
      2. We do this by being faithful in giving to the Kingdom.
   C. We understand faith in our secular lives.
      1. It is planting a seed in the ground.
      2. It is riding in an airplane.
   D. In our spiritual lives faith is just the same.
      1. It is writing a check for our tithes.
      2. It is telling someone that Jesus loves him or her.
      3. It is trusting the truths of the Bible to give direction to our lives.
      4. It is praying and leaving the burden at the altar.

Conclusion
   A. "Without faith it is impossible to please God" (Heb. 11:6).
   B. "If [faith] is not accompanied by action, [it] is dead" (James 2:17).
   C. Mix the energy of your life with what you say you believe, and bring glory to God.

Sinners, Servants, or Sons?

Romans 8:12-17

Introduction
A. In Romans Paul describes the beautiful life God had in mind for people when He created them.
   1. In chapter 5 Paul describes the problem and the cure.
   2. In 6:11-14 Paul gives us the choice we must make.
   3. In chapter 7 Paul pictures the struggle of a person with a mixed nature.
   4. In chapter 8 Paul gives God's plan for His people.
   5. Read the scripture, Rom. 8:12-17.
B. Every person falls into one of three categories.
   1. Sinners—rebels against God
   2. Servants—purchased by His blood and belonging to Him
   3. Sons (or daughters)—those who truly love the Father and desire to please Him
C. There are big differences between these groups.
   1. Sinners are limited to the transient peace the world gives.
   2. Servants are limited to the action they believe their Master wants.
   3. Sons (or daughters) live in total freedom because of the love of the Father.
D. We determine which relationship we have.

I. Look at the Nature of the Sinful Life as Described in John 8:19-24
A. Jesus is dialoging with the Pharisees after they brought a woman to Him that had been caught in the act of adultery (vv. 1-22).
   1. The Pharisees were attacking Jesus' credibility.
   2. Jesus set the record straight (vv. 12-18).
B. Sinners are bound by the conditions of this world (v. 23).
   1. They are more interested in what feels good than what is right.

        2. They can justify actions to themselves but not to God.
        3. They have a false sense of freedom.
    C. Jesus paid the price to purchase freedom for all of sin's slaves.

II. **Look at the Nature of the Servant's Life as Described in Rom. 6:16-22**
    A. Paul says that everyone is a servant of something (v. 16). It is possible to be a servant of the Lord.
    B. Look at the role of a servant.
        1. A servant is obedient and does what he or she is told.
        2. A servant lives in fear of displeasing his or her Master.
        3. A servant is rewarded for well doing and punished for wrongdoing.
        4. A servant lives outside of the Father's house and has limited provisions.

III. **Look at the Nature of the Son's Life as Described in 2 Cor. 6:13-18**
    A. Let's examine the position of the sons (Rom. 8:15-17).
        1. The sons live in absolute confidence because of their relationship with their Father.
        2. All of the resources of the Father are available to the sons.
        3. Sinners and servants do not know this confidence.
    B. Paul tells us in 2 Cor. 6:13-18 how to be a son.
        1. Verse 13 says, "Open your heart to what I say."
        2. Verse 14 says, "Separate yourself from the world."
        3. Let Him fill you with himself.

Conclusion
    A. It is our glorious privilege to be the sons and daughters of God. This is not a difficult condition but a happy one.
    B. Everyone chooses the life of sin, servanthood, or sonship.
    C. Which will you choose?